D0344212

Para||el History

One Period | Global Developments | Side by Side

❋ THE NINETEENTH- ❋
CENTURY WORLD

1800 - 1900

Alex Woolf

Illustrated by Victor Beuren

W

FRANKLIN WATTS
LONDON•SYDNEY

Franklin Watts
First published in Great Britain in 2017
by The Watts Publishing Group

Copyright © The Watts Publishing Group 2017

Credits
Artwork by Victor Beuren
Design: Collaborate Agency
Editor: Nicola Edwards

ISBN 978 1 4451 5742 9

Printed in China

Franklin Watts
An imprint of
Hachette Children's Group
Part of The Watts Publishing Group
Carmelite House
50 Victoria Embankment
London EC4Y 0DZ

An Hachette UK Company
www.hachette.co.uk

www.franklinwatts.co.uk

MIX
Paper from
responsible sources
FSC® C104740
FSC
www.fsc.org

❊ CONTENTS ❊

❈ INTRODUCTION ❈

The nineteenth century was an era of extraordinary social and political change. It witnessed the end of absolute monarchy and the rise of nationalism (allegiance to one's country). The Spanish Empire collapsed, and the Ottoman Empire continued to decline, as peoples within them fought for nationhood. Meanwhile, the USA, Russia and Japan grew more powerful, and the British Empire reached its zenith – by the end of the century, it ruled a quarter of the world's population.

Colour Key
- Africa
- Americas
- Asia
- Europe
- Australia and Oceania

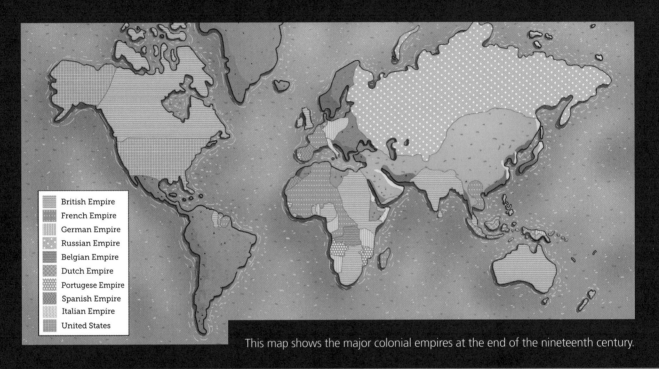

- British Empire
- French Empire
- German Empire
- Russian Empire
- Belgian Empire
- Dutch Empire
- Portugese Empire
- Spanish Empire
- Italian Empire
- United States

This map shows the major colonial empires at the end of the nineteenth century.

The French Revolution

The trigger for a century of upheaval came in 1789. Angered by poverty and food shortages, the people of France overthrew their king. A new National Assembly was formed, publishing a *Declaration of the Rights of Man*, proclaiming that power rested with the people. The revolution grew more violent. The king and many nobles were beheaded. It ended, finally, with the rise to power of a young military leader, Napoleon.

The Bastille fortress, hated symbol of the old regime, was stormed in July 1789.

Science and industry

In the course of this century, scientists and engineers in Europe and the USA transformed the world. This was the beginning of mass communication, with the development of the telegraph, the telephone and radio. Railways shortened journey times. Steam-powered machines gave rise to factories and an Industrial Revolution that changed forever the way humans lived and worked.

Children as young as five or six were often employed in factories.

In 1837, American innovator Samuel Morse invented the telegraph, the first mass communication device.

Social change

Industrialisation spread across the world and led to far-reaching changes in society. A new elite of industrialists, business and professional people – the 'middle classes' – replaced the old aristocracy. Millions of rural labourers moved to towns and cities to work in factories. For factory workers, conditions were often terrible, leading to demands for social reform and the rise of trade unions.

Britain fought two wars with the Qing dynasty to force China to open itself up to trade.

Asia and the Pacific

The European powers ruled over India and much of South-East Asia while wielding increasing influence in China. The British founded new colonies in Australia and New Zealand. With China on the wane, the century witnessed the rise of a new power in East Asia: Japan.

✦ REVOLUTIONS ✦

The nationalist upsurge led to popular revolts and revolutions in different parts of the world. Many of these were inspired by the American and French Revolutions, and the Enlightenment ideals of liberty, democracy and constitutional government. Some revolutions failed, but others led to the formation of new and independent nation states.

Revolutionaries in Berlin in March 1848.

During the Haitian Revolution, French troops fought against rebel slaves.

Europe

In 1830, a revolution in France overthrew King Charles X. This inspired nationalist uprisings in Italy and Germany, later suppressed. In 1848, another flurry of revolutions erupted: France became a republic, and nationalists briefly overturned Austrian rule in parts of central Europe. But the most significant consequence of nationalism was the emergence of the unified nation states of Italy and Germany.

Haiti

In the French colony of Saint-Domingue, the slaves rose up and overthrew their masters to found the sovereign nation of Haiti. The Haitian Revolution is the only example of a successful slave uprising leading to the establishment of a slave-free society ruled by non-whites. It sent shockwaves through the slave-owning colonies of the New World.

1791–1804 Haitian Revolution	**1816** Argentina declares independence	**1825** Peru declares independence. Upper Peru renames itself Bolivia after Simón Bolívar
Paraguay declares independence **1811**	Uruguay achieves independence **1828**	Louis-Philippe of France abdicates in favour of President Louis Napoleon. Revolutions in Hungary, Croatia and Czech lands **1848**
	European revolutions are suppressed, but led to creation of independent Belgium **1830–1831**	

Central America

The Mexican war of independence, led by Miguel Hidalgo, broke out in 1810. Hidalgo was executed in 1811, and military commander Agustín Iturbide took over the leadership. By 1822, he had driven the Spanish royalists out of the country. The other Central American colonies also declared independence around this time.

Agustín Iturbide founded the Mexican Empire in 1822, with himself as emperor.

South America

Simón Bolívar led the struggle to free the northern colonies of South America. The struggle in the south was led by José de San Martín. By 1826, the last of the Spanish royalists had been driven out of mainland South and Central America. Brazil became an independent country in 1822.

Simón Bolívar meets José de San Martín in Ecuador, 1822.

| 1852 | Louis Napoleon declares himself emperor and suppresses dissent. Austrian Habsburgs crush nationalist rebels in their territories |

| 1865 – 1871 | Unification of Germany |

| 1859 – 1870 | Unification of Italy |

1860   1870   1880   1890   1900

❧ THE RISE OF THE NATION STATE ❧

New ideas were unleashed by the French Revolution, which quickly spread across Europe and the Americas. People now demanded to live in more equal societies. They wanted governments that guaranteed their rights as citizens. Above all, people wished to live in independent states with a common language and culture – in other words, nations. This growing feeling of nationalism led, in many parts of the world, to demands for political independence.

In the Greek War of Independence, the nationalists used weapons including pistols, muskets and swords.

The great powers met in 1815 to divide up Europe between them.

Europe

Napoleon's wars of conquest (1803–1815) briefly united much of Europe under a French Empire. After his defeat, the great powers (Austria, Prussia, Russia and Britain) ignored smaller countries' demands for independence. This led to nationalist uprisings in southern Italy and Spain, which were brutally suppressed.

Ottoman Empire

The declining Ottoman Empire was not strong enough to contain nationalist struggles within its borders. After uprisings in Serbia, Moldavia and Wallachia, the Ottomans offered these territories some self-rule. In 1821, a revolt broke out in Greece. After a long fight, the Ottomans were forced to accept Greek independence.

1803-1815 Napoleon's wars of conquest	*1821–1832* Greek War of Independence	
Beginning of Mexico's War of Independence *1810*	*1810-1822* Mexico's War of Independence	*1826* The last Spanish royalists are driven out of South America
Nationalist uprising in southern Italy *1820*	*1822* Nationalist uprising in Spain	The Dutch recognise Belgian independence *1839*

The Indian Mutiny was started by soldiers in the East India Company's army.

India

The British East India Company steadily extended its control over India. The Company upset many Indians with its ban on local customs and its policy of Christian conversion. The Indians rose in rebellion in 1857. The 'Indian Mutiny' was defeated, but awoke a desire among many Indians for independence. They founded an organisation, the Indian National Congress, to fight for this cause.

Latin America

By the start of the nineteenth century, creoles (people of Spanish descent) in the American colonies had grown resentful of Spanish authority. Spain demanded ever more revenue, excluded them from government jobs, and denied them the power to trade. The creoles began to want independence from Spain. When Napoleon deposed the Spanish king in 1808, and replaced him with his brother, wars of independence broke out across Latin America.

A priest, Miguel Hidalgo, led the Mexican war of independence.

1857 Indian Mutiny

1885 Indian National Congress is founded

1878 Montenegro, Romania and Serbia win independence from the Ottoman Empire

1860 .... 1870 .... 1880 .... 1890 1900

❀ THE GROWTH OF INDUSTRY ❀

In the eighteenth century, most goods were produced by hand in homes or small workshops. Merchants would hand raw materials such as cotton or wool to workers, then collect the finished products. With the invention of steam-driven machines, workers, materials and machines were brought together in factories. Production was made more efficient by breaking it down into smaller tasks that workers could specialise in. This was the beginning of the Industrial Revolution.

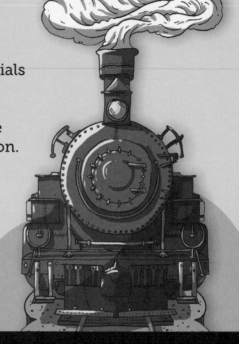

The steam locomotive brought faster transportation of goods and raw materials.

Britain

The Industrial Revolution began in Britain during the second half of the eighteenth century. Britain had huge coal reserves to power its machines, and iron ore to make machine parts, bridges, ships and trains. It had access to raw materials from its colonies, where it could also sell its products. Britain became known as the 'workshop of the world'.

The Industrial Revolution began in the textile mills of northern England.

Continental Europe

In the 1830s, Belgium became the second country to industrialise, as the cities of Ghent, Liege and Verviers became major centres of textile production. The German states followed. From the mid-nineteenth century, European countries began reducing import taxes, ushering in a new era of free trade.

Britain is producing more coal, iron and textiles than the rest of Europe combined — *1815*

The first German railway opens — *1835*

1846 — Britain drops its import tax on corn, boosting trade

1825 — The first railway opens in Britain

1830–1850 — Coal production doubles in the German states

USA

From 1865, a 'Second Industrial Revolution' began, this one led by the USA. The development of steel and electric power boosted productivity, and mechanisation spread to the food, clothing and transport industries. The USA experienced a so-called 'Gilded Age', as labour shortages led to higher wages and a huge influx of immigrants.

American cities like New York experienced massive population growth as European immigrants flooded in to fill the job vacancies.

Japanese train track increased from 29 km to 3,400 km in just 22 years between 1872 and 1894.

Japan

The traditional political system of Japan, dominated by shoguns (military commanders) and daimyo (nobles), broke down in 1868 in a revolution known as the Meiji Restoration. The new rulers were politicians from the Satsuma and Chōshū Domains, who took power under the nominal rule of Emperor Meiji. They embarked on a massive industrialisation programme. Japan imported Western steam engines, cotton-spinning mills and steel. By the 1890s Japan had joined the ranks of the leading industrial nations.

1856 Britain's Henry Bessemer pioneers the manufacture of steel from iron ore

1860–1880 US railway triples in size, opening up new areas for farming

1890 Japan becomes a leading industrial nation after importing Western technology

1860   1870   1880   1890   1900

❋ COLONIALISM ❋

The Industrial Revolution sparked a new wave of colonialism in the nineteenth century. In search of new markets for their goods, cheap sources of raw materials and areas to settle their populations, the European powers expanded further into India, South-East Asia, Australia, New Zealand and Africa.

India

The British East India Company did not plan to conquer India. Territories were only captured to protect the Company's interests. Yet by 1856, the entire Indian subcontinent was ruled by the Company or loyal local rulers. After the Indian Mutiny, the British government began ruling India directly in a period known as the Raj. Railway and telegraph networks were built, and universities founded.

Thousands of Indian men served as soldiers defending the British Empire.

The Governor-General's palace in Saigon, Indochina, which was ruled by France from the 1860s.

South-East Asia

From 1870, Western intervention intensified, and by 1900 almost the entire region had been colonised, with Siam (modern Thailand) the last independent state. The British controlled the Malacca Straits, the Malay Peninsula, North Borneo and Burma. The Dutch had to fight local rebellions to hold onto their territory on Sumatra and Java. New Guinea was shared by Germany, the Netherlands and Britain, while the USA took over the Philippines in 1898.

1814 British annex Cape Colony, driving out the Afrikaner (Dutch) settlers, who founded new colonies: Orange Free State and Transvaal

British capture Singapore *1819*

English is made the language of education in India *1835*

1830 France conquers northern Algeria

Discovery of gold in Australia *1851*

Africa

For most of the century, European colonies were dotted around the African coastline. From 1880, a 'scramble for Africa' began, and by 1914, virtually the entire continent had been colonised by European powers such as Britain, France, Belgium, Portugal and Germany. Superior weaponry and military training made this possible, and many African rulers were happy to help the Europeans if it meant defeat for their traditional enemies.

Newspaper cartoons depicted European leaders dividing up territory in Africa as a cake to be shared among them.

As British settlers expanded their territory in Australia, they came into conflict with Australian Aboriginal people.

Australia

The Europeans 'discovered' Australia in the seventeenth century. The British established a penal colony at Port Jackson (modern Sydney) in 1788, and began shipping convicts there. Free settlers began arriving from the 1830s. The discovery of gold transformed the colony. The population expanded from 405,000 in 1850 to four million in 1900.

1876 British monarch, Queen Victoria, is given title Empress of India

1858 French capture Saigon and Da Nang in Indochina (modern Vietnam)

1884–5 Berlin Conference: representatives of 15 European nations meet to settle rival claims in Africa

1860   1870   1880   1890   1900

✳ EXPLORATION ✳

During the nineteenth century, the vast interiors of North America, Africa and Australia were explored and mapped by Europeans. Their motives varied. Some desired land for grazing and settlement. Others were driven by scientific interest, religious zeal or simply a spirit of adventure.

USA

In 1800, the USA was a small nation perched on the east coast of North America. Over the next century, it expanded westward, acquiring territory from France, Spain and Mexico. Before the new land could be settled, it had to be explored and mapped. Meriwether Lewis and William Clark led an expedition that established a route to the Pacific coast and inspired an era of exploration. By the 1860s, settlers had begun to occupy the Great Plains west of the Mississippi.

Alexander Mackenzie made the first east-to-west crossing of North America.

On their travels, Lewis and Clark were helped by Native Americans, such as Sacagawea of the Lemhi Shoshone tribe.

Canada

In the early nineteenth century, rival companies fought for control of Canada's fur trade. This spurred exploration of Canada's west, as traders searched for new routes and suppliers. Alexander Mackenzie, Simon Fraser and David Thompson explored and mapped the Western territories as far as the Pacific and the Arctic Oceans.

 1804–6 American explorers Lewis and Clark journey across the western regions of North America

1804–7 American Zebulon Pike explores Colorado and New Mexico

1808 American Simon Fraser explores Fraser River, Canada

Pioneers start travelling west from Missouri to the Pacific on the 'Oregon Trail' **1843**

1827–8 René Caillié's expedition in West Africa

Africa

From the 1820s European explorers began to journey into the African interior. Frenchman René Caillié was probably the first European to visit Timbuktu. Scottish explorer David Livingstone travelled through Central and Southern Africa. His discoveries inspired new expeditions, seeking the sources of the Nile, Congo, Zambezi and Niger rivers. The charting of the interior helped establish colonial boundaries during the 'scramble for Africa' (see page 13).

René Caillié explored West Africa dressed as an Arab.

Burke and Wills died on their return journey across Australia.

Australia

Navigator Matthew Flinders was the first to circumnavigate Australia in 1802–3. Harsh conditions made exploring the interior more challenging. Robert O'Hara Burke and William John Wills were the first to traverse the entire continent, crossing south to north in 1860–1. Expeditions in the 1870s helped open up parts of Western Australia for grazing.

1860 — Scottish explorer John Stuart finds Australia's geographic centre

1851–71 — David Livingstone's expeditions in Africa

WAR AND CONFLICT

Industrialisation and technology changed warfare in the nineteenth century. It became possible to move large numbers of troops rapidly on railroads, and to communicate over long distances via telegraph. Guns and artillery were developed that could shoot further and more accurately than ever before. Navies began using iron-hulled warships and even the first submarines.

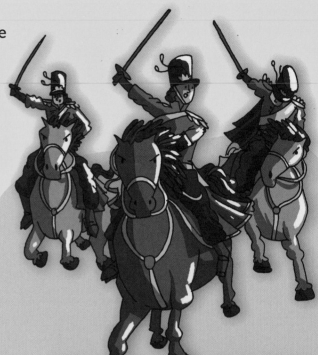

The Charge of the Light Brigade, a doomed cavalry charge by the British in the Crimean War.

One of Napoleon's greatest victories was at Austerlitz, in December 1805.

Europe

From 1803 to 1815, Europe was almost constantly at war as the French Empire under Napoleon fought with various European powers, led by Britain, for control of the continent. Napoleon was a brilliant strategist, able to outwit his enemies with the speed of his troop movements and the timing of his attacks.

Crimea

In the Crimean War, Russia fought an alliance of the Ottoman Empire, Britain and France. The conflict saw the introduction of trench warfare, long-range artillery, rifles, armoured warships, submarine mines and the telegraph. The human cost of mechanised warfare was immense, with more than one million people killed.

Battle of Jena: Napoleon defeats Prussian army

October 1806

1815 Napoleon faces his final defeat at Waterloo

July 1809 Battle of Wagram: Napoleon defeats Austrian army

1812 Napoleon over-reaches himself with disastrous invasion of Russia

1838 Boers (Dutch settlers in southern Africa) defeat the Zulus in the Battles of Italeni and Blood River

1804 – 1810 In the Fulani War in West Africa, the Fulani army of Usman dan Fodio defeats the Hausa kingdoms

USA

The American Civil War began when the southern states broke away from the USA because they wanted to maintain slavery. For three years, the Confederate (southern) army defended itself against Union army attacks in a series of bloody battles. In May 1865, the Confederacy surrendered. Victory for the North preserved the USA as one nation and ended slavery, but it came at the cost of 625,000 lives.

Union and Confederate armies clash in the American Civil War.

Japanese troops in the war with China. The war demonstrated the superiority of Japanese forces after their adoption Western-style military tactics and training.

East Asia

Japan went to war with China in August 1894, mainly over control of Korea. Japan's forces were victorious in a string of battles on land and sea, and in February 1895, China surrendered. The war was a humiliating blow for China's Qing dynasty, and proved that Japan was now the dominant military power in East Asia.

1853–1856 Crimean War	*10 May 1865* American Civil War ends	*16 January 1878* Turkish steamer *Intibah* is first vessel to be sunk by a self-propelled torpedo, which was launched by a Russian torpedo boat during the Turko-Russian War of 1877-8

February 1864 First successful submarine attack in wartime when *H. L. Hunley* sinks frigate *USS Housatonic*

12 April 1861 Confederate army attack on Fort Sumter in Charleston Harbor triggers American Civil War

1879 The Xhosa Wars (which began in 1779) end with the takeover of Xhosa territory in southern Africa by the British

March 1862 Battle of Hampton Roads (American Civil War) proves effectiveness of ironclad warships, changing naval warfare

1889–1896 Ethiopians defeat Italians at Battle of Adwa during First Italo-Ethiopian War

1860   1870   1880   1890   1900

SCIENCE AND TECHNOLOGY

In the nineteenth century, science became a professional discipline. It began to divide into specialised fields, like physics, chemistry and biology. Key advances were made in all areas, especially by scientists (a word coined in 1834) working in Britain, the USA, France and Germany.

Edison demonstrated his electric light bulb on 31 December 1879.

Charles Darwin published his theory of evolution in his book *On the Origin of Species* (1859).

Britain

John Dalton proposed that matter is made up of tiny, indivisible atoms. Michael Faraday showed that a magnet can produce electricity. James Clerk Maxwell demonstrated that electricity and magnetism were different forms of the same thing, and light is an electromagnetic wave. Charles Darwin theorised that species evolve over time through a process called natural selection.

USA

Numerous technological advances were made by US inventors during the nineteenth century. Joseph Henry constructed the world's first electric motor. Scottish-born Alexander Graham Bell invented the telephone. Thomas Edison patented over 1,000 inventions, including the electric light bulb and the phonograph.

Heinrich Hertz used this device to prove that electric sparks could jump across a gap in a circuit.

Germany

Friedrich Wöhler isolated the element aluminium in 1827. In 1838, astronomer Friedrich Bessel became the first to measure the distance to a star. In 1847, Hermann von Helmholtz, a physicist, formulated the law of the Conservation of Energy, which states that energy is never lost but just changes from one form to another. In 1888, Heinrich Hertz proved the existence of the electromagnetic waves predicted by James Clerk Maxwell.

Marie Curie won two Nobel Prizes for her work on radioactivity.

France

Nicéphore Niépce pioneered photography in the 1820s, and Louis Le Prince shot the first motion picture in 1888. In 1896, Henri Becquerel discovered radioactivity. Then, in 1898, Polish-born Marie Curie and her husband Pierre discovered the radioactive element radium.

MEDICINE

Major progress was made in the diagnosis and treatment of disease during the century. New medical devices were developed, including the stethoscope, kymograph (for measuring the pulse) and electrocardiograph (for measuring heart activity). At the same time, public health faced new challenges: the Industrial Revolution drew millions into cities, leading to the faster spread of diseases, such as cholera, smallpox and typhus. Some factory workers were exposed to dangerous chemicals, causing skin and lung disorders.

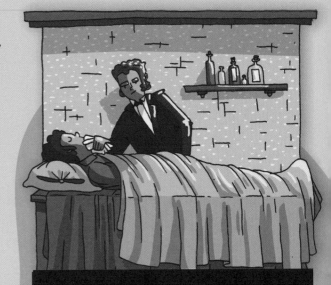

Crawford Long's pioneering work with ether enabled surgeons to attempt operations that were previously impossible.

Pasteur invented a process of heating liquids to kill bacteria, known today as 'pasteurisation'.

France

In a series of experiments between 1857 and 1863, Louis Pasteur proved that germs cause disease. The bacteria that cause bubonic plague was discovered by another Frenchman, Alexandre Yersin. He helped Pasteur develop a vaccine for the disease rabies, in 1885. In 1884, French biologist Charles Chamberland discovered viruses.

USA

Americans pioneered the use of anaesthetics (pain blockers) for surgery. Crawford Long was the first to use ether to anaesthetise a patient. Medical technology improved: George Green invented the electric dental drill in 1875. William Upjohn invented the dissolvable pill in 1884, and William Halsted invented the latex surgical glove in 1894, making surgery safer.

Joseph Jackson Lister, the father of Joseph Lister, invents the multi-lens microscope, allowing doctors to see microorganisms — 1826

Herman von Helmholtz (see page 19) invents the ophthalmoscope (a device for looking inside the human eye) — 1851

Hungarian surgeon Ignaz Semmelweis cuts death rate on maternity ward by making doctors wash their hands — 1847

1822 — American surgeon William Beaumont learns about the digestive system by studying a man with a hole in his stomach

Joseph Lister's sterilisation procedures dramatically cut death rates for surgery.

Britain

In 1847, James Simpson discovered another anaesthetic – chloroform. And in the 1860s the surgeon Joseph Lister was inspired by Pasteur's germ theory to sterilize instruments and bandages with carbolic acid. In 1876 Patrick Manson discovered that mosquitoes can be vectors (carriers) for disease.

Germany

In 1839, Theodor Schwann worked out that all plant and animal matter was made up of cells, the basic units of body tissue. Building on Schwann's work, physician Rudolf Virchow showed how all diseases arise from disorders in cells. This helped discredit the humour theory – that illness is caused by an imbalance in the four humours: blood, yellow bile, black bile and phlegm.

Theodor Schwann showed that all life begins with a single cell.

COMMUNICATION AND TRANSPORT

The world shrank in the nineteenth century, thanks to our discovery of new ways to move and communicate at speed over distance. Steam locomotives and steamships cut travel times, and the electric telegraph enabled messages to be sent across continents in minutes. Towards the end of the century, new inventions like the telephone, radio and motor car were set to transform the world yet again.

Bell makes the first two-way long-distance telephone call between Cambridge and Boston, Massachusetts.

The Stockton and Darlington Railway was 40 km long.

Britain

The steam locomotive was invented in Britain in the early nineteenth century by pioneers including Richard Trevithick and George Stephenson. The Stockton and Darlington Railway, the world's first public steam railway, opened in 1825. The world's first underground railway was built in London in 1863. Electric underground trains began running in the capital in 1890.

USA

Samuel Morse created the telegraph, which used electricity to transmit coded messages along a wire. He developed Morse Code, a system using dots and dashes to represent text. Alexander Graham Bell discovered a way of sending speech over wires by turning sounds into electrical signals, then back into sounds. He patented his 'telephone' in 1876.

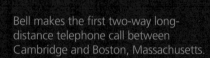

Steamships begin crossing the English Channel — 1815

The steamship Sirius, built in Scotland, crosses the Atlantic from Cork, Ireland, to New York City, USA, in just 19 days — 1838

American physicist Joseph Henry sends an electric current along 1.6 km of wire — 1830

1840 British postal service starts using stamps

Samuel Morse invents the electric telegraph — 1837

1840s Boom in railway building in Britain

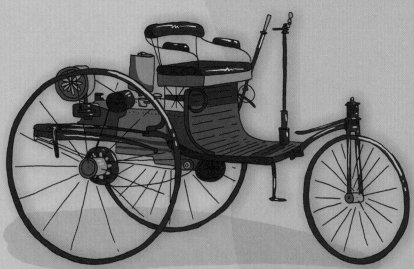

Germany

There were attempts to create powered vehicles dating back to the eighteenth century, but the inventor of the first practical automobile was German engineer Karl Benz. In 1885, he built a petrol-powered vehicle with a two-stroke piston engine. His wife Bertha made the first long-distance car journey in 1888. She drove 106 km, proving its suitability for daily use. By 1900, mass production of automobiles had begun in France and the USA.

The Benz Patent-Motorwagen, the world's first practical car.

Italy

Radio had many pioneers, including Heinrich Hertz, Oliver Lodge and Nikola Tesla. But the man who put all these innovations together to create 'wireless telegraphy' (the sending of messages through the air, using radio waves) was Italian physicist Guglielmo Marconi. In 1895, Marconi built the first long-distance radio transmitter and receiver. Four years later, he sent a wireless message across the English Channel.

Guglielmo Marconi was awarded the 1909 Nobel Prize in physics (shared with German inventor Karl Braun) for his contributions to radio technology.

1866 First successful transatlantic telegraph cable laid between Europe and North America

1875 Alexander Graham Bell manages to transmit a sound over a wire

1877 First telephone switchboard begins operating in Boston, USA

1860   1870   1880   1890   1900

ART

Nineteenth-century art reflected the mood of the times. Nationalism, nostalgia and a desire for emotional truth all found expression in painting. Artists no longer produced work solely for the Church or wealthy patrons, but for display to the public, so were more free to attempt bold, new styles. Paint, pre-mixed in a wide variety of colours, became available in tubes, which artists could carry around with them.

Claude Monet's painting *Impression, Sunrise* gave its name to a new style: Impressionism.

France

Romanticism, which emphasised emotion and glorified nature and the individual, was the dominant movement of the early nineteenth century. Delacroix and Géricault painted dramatic, exotic scenes. In the mid-nineteenth century, Courbet pioneered Realism, reacting against idealistic art. In the 1870s, the impressionists, Monet, Renoir and Degas, tried to capture the shifting effects of light and colour.

Russia

The art movement Peredvizhniki (Wanderers) began as a protest against the Imperial Academy of Arts and its emphasis on history painting. Peredvizhniki painted realistic views of contemporary life in Russia. The first exhibition opened to huge acclaim and attracted thousands of visitors. By the 1880s, the paintings of this 'protest movement' were being purchased by the tsar's family.

The Peredvizhniki travelled from city to city, exhibiting their paintings, such as *Unknown Woman* by Ivan Kramskoi.

1750–1850 Neoclassical art revived Greco-Roman styles

1780–1850 Romanticism celebrated human imagination, individuality and emotion

1820 Founding of US art movement the Hudson River School, a group of landscape artists whose paintings offered a realistic, detailed and sometimes romanticised portrayal of nature

1848 Founding of Pre-Raphaelite Brotherhood by Dante Gabriel Rossetti, William Holman Hunt and John Everett Millais

Britain

The Romantic movement of British art was led by Turner and Constable. Turner's style changed, however, and the wild, almost abstract landscapes of his later career influenced the French impressionists. Another important movement was the Pre-Raphaelite Brotherhood: artists such as Millais and Rossetti painted religious and literary subjects in a minutely detailed style.

Latin America

In the years after their countries gained independence, Latin American artists tried to forge a new style of art, blending native traditions with those from Europe. These artists were known as costumbristas. Influenced by the European romantic style, painters like Pueyrredón, Pinto and Arrieta painted lush, colourful landscapes and scenes of everyday life.

One of the paintings by Argentinian artist Prilidiano Pueyrredón was entitled *A Stop at the Grocery Store*.

1870 Peredvizhniki movement is formed in Russia

1848–1900 Realist artists try to represent people and things as they actually are

1865–1885 Impressionist painters capture the fleeting effects of natural light

Post-impressionist artists react against the naturalism of Impressionism in their exploration of colour, line and form
1885–1910

1860   1870   1880   1890   1900

✤ ARCHITECTURE ✤

The industrial age required new kinds of buildings, including factories, railway stations, warehouses, offices, banks and department stores. Vast numbers of low-cost homes were needed to house workers in rapidly expanding cities. Advances in cast-iron manufacture and mass-produced glass allowed the creation of enormous structures.

Britain

Revival movements dominated the early part of the century. The Houses of Parliament, begun in 1837, were rebuilt in a medieval Gothic style, while the British Museum was built in 'Greek Revival', inspired by ancient Greek temples. In 1851, an enormous, futuristic, iron-and-glass structure, the Crystal Palace, was erected to house London's Great Exhibition.

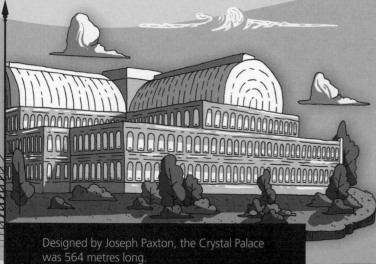

Designed by Joseph Paxton, the Crystal Palace was 564 metres long.

France

Around the time the Crystal Palace was being built, Henri Labrouste designed an impressive iron-and-glass library, the Bibliothèque Sainte-Geneviève, in Paris. Charles Garnier looked back in time when he designed the famous Palais Garnier opera house, which was built between 1861 and 1875, blending earlier architectural styles such as Baroque and Renaissance.

The Palais Garnier is full of elaborate friezes, columns and statues.

1800 — United States Capitol, where the US Congress meets, was designed in the Neoclassical style by William Thornton

1824 — The Second Bank of the United States in Philadelphia was designed by William Strickland in Greek Revival style

The Bibliothèque Sainte-Geneviève in Paris — 1850

USA

In the closing decades of the century, the Americans invented a brand new kind of building: the skyscraper. The development of steel-frame construction and the safety elevator made it possible to build these tall, multi-storey buildings. Skyscrapers were supported by a steel frame from which the walls were hung like curtains.

The Home Insurance Building in Chicago – the world's first skyscraper. Its architect, William Le Baron Jenney, studied alongside Gustave Eiffel in Paris.

Nippon Kangyo Bank (1899), designed by Tsumaki Yorinaka, a student of Ende and Böckmann.

Japan

The Meiji government invited Western architects to share their expertise. English architect Josiah Conder adapted different European styles with his Bank of Japan (1896). German architects Hermann Ende and Wilhelm Böckmann combined the grand scale of Western buildings with traditional Japanese elements, such as tiled, gabled roofs and curved, overhanging eaves.

1865 Completion of Houses of Parliament

1885 The Home Insurance Building, Chicago, the world's first skyscraper, designed by William Le Baron Jenney

1860   1870   1880   1890   1900

LITERATURE

As it did with art, Romanticism dominated the literature of the early part of the century. This was the era when the novel established itself as a popular form of fiction. In the latter half of the century, new genres of novel emerged, such as science fantasy and detective stories.

French writer Dumas wrote the classic, *The Three Musketeers* (1844).

British writer Arthur Conan Doyle invented his famous fictional detective Sherlock Holmes in 1887.

France

The great French writers of the Romantic era, such as Victor Hugo and Alexandre Dumas, enjoyed international prestige. Mid-century, Realism emerged in reaction to Romanticism. The novels of Stendhal and Balzac addressed issues of contemporary society. From the 1860s, 'naturalist' writers such as de Maupassant and Zola showed characters controlled by their birth and circumstances.

Britain

British Romantic poets, such as Wordsworth, Shelley and Keats, reacted against industrialisation with their nature poems, highlighting the healing power of the imagination. Jane Austen's novels were famed for their dry wit and social observation. Charles Dickens' novels, while loved for their humour, focused attention on urban poverty. The Brontë sisters broke new ground with their vivid, passionate novels from a woman's perspective.

1802–1822

Hizakurige ('Shank's Mare') by Ikku Jippensha, a famous Japanese comic novel, published in 12 parts

The Last of the Mohicans by James Fenimore Cooper 1826

Frankenstein by Mary Shelley 1818

Pride and Prejudice by Jane Austen 1820

The Legend of Sleepy Hollow, a short story by Washington Irving 1820

The Fall of the House of Usher, a short story by Edgar Allen Poe 1839

Eugene Onegin, a novel in verse, by Alexander Pushkin 1833

Diary of a Madman, a short story by Nikolai Gogol 1835

Oliver Twist by Charles Dickens 1838

Jane Eyre by Charlotte Brontë and *Wuthering Heights* by Emily Brontë 1847

1843 *Sita Swayamvar* by Vishnudas Bhave is the first Marathi-language play

Uncle Tom's Cabin was an anti-slavery classic by American writer Harriet Beecher Stowe.

USA

A uniquely American style of literature emerged in the nineteenth century. Key writers included Washington Irving, James Fenimore Cooper and author of mysteries, Edgar Allan Poe. Mark Twain wrote humorous stories involving characters with distinctively American speech styles. *Moby-Dick* by Herman Melville was a whale-hunting adventure published in 1851 that explored themes of obsession and the nature of evil.

Leo Tolstoy was the author of *War and Peace*, which is regarded as one if the greatest novels ever written.

Russia

The nineteenth century is often referred to as the 'Golden Era' of Russian literature. Alexander Pushkin was the foremost romantic poet, credited with introducing a new level of artistry into the Russian language. Novelists, including Gogol, Tolstoy, Turgenev and Dostoyevsky, wrote works of international renown. Anton Chekhov became one of the world's leading writers of plays and short stories.

1851 *Moby-Dick* by Herman Melville

1862 *Les Miserables* by Victor Hugo

1878 *The Story of Hero Boys and Hero Girls* by Yanbei Xianren, a famous Qing dynasty novel

1856 *Madame Bovary* by Gustave Flaubert

1869 *War and Peace* by Leo Tolstoy

The Seagull, a play by Anton Chekhov 1896

1862 *Fathers and Sons* by Ivan Turgenev

1880 *The Brothers Karamazov* by Fyodor Dostoyevsky

1852 *Uncle Tom's Cabin* by Harriet Beecher Stowe

1897 *Dracula* by Bram Stoker

1860   1870   1880   1890   1900

GLOSSARY

absolute monarchy
A system of government in which the monarch has supreme authority and is not restricted by written laws, assemblies or customs.

annex
Add (territory) to one's own territory, usually by force.

aristocracy
The highest class in certain societies, made up of people of noble birth.

artillery
Heavy guns that are used in land warfare.

bacteria
Plural of bacterium, a type of microorganism, some of which can cause disease.

biopsy
An examination of tissue removed from a living person to discover the presence, cause or extent of a disease.

cast iron
A hard alloy (a metal combining two or more elements) of iron and carbon, which can be cast in a mould.

coined
Invented (a new word or phrase).

colonialism
The policy of acquiring control of another country and occupying it with settlers.

colony
A country or territory under the political control of another country and occupied by settlers from that country.

democracy
A system of government under which the leaders have been elected freely by the citizens.

diagnosis
The identification of an illness.

dissent
The holding or expression of opinions that disagree with those officially held.

dynasty
A line of hereditary rulers of a country.

East India Company
A trading company founded in England in 1600 to develop trade and commerce with South-East Asia and India.

electromagnetic wave
An energy wave produced by the interaction of electric and magnetic fields. They include radio waves, X-rays and visible light.

Enlightenment
A European intellectual movement of the late seventeenth and eighteenth centuries, which emphasises reason and the freedom of the individual rather than tradition.

free trade
International trade that is free of tariffs (taxes on imports or exports) or other restrictions.

Gothic (architecture)
A style characterised by pointed arches, curved vaults, large windows and ornate stonework.

Great Exhibition
A display of objects from around the world, which opened in 1851 in London's Hyde Park. The exhibits were arranged into four main categories: machinery, manufactures, fine arts and raw materials.

import taxes
Money that must be paid to the government of a country in order to sell goods to that country.

Indian subcontinent
The great peninsula of southern Asia that comprises modern-day India, Pakistan and Bangladesh.

industrialist
Someone involved in the ownership and management of industry.

Industrial Revolution
The rapid development of industry that began in Britain in the late eighteenth century, involving steam-powered machinery, the growth of factories and the mass production of manufactured goods.

influx
The arrival of large numbers (of people).

microorganism
A microscopic organism, such as a bacterium or virus.

natural selection
The process by which organisms better adapted to their environment tend to survive and produce more offspring.

patent (verb)
Obtain a patent, or licence, for an invention, giving the inventor the right for a set period of time to make, use and sell it.

penal colony
A settlement in a remote location to which prisoners are sent.

phonograph
An early form of gramophone using cylinders, able to record as well as reproduce sound.

radioactivity
Energy in the form of streams of particles caused by the decay of unstable atoms.

Romanticism
A movement in the arts and literature beginning in the late eighteenth century, emphasising inspiration and the importance of the individual.

royalist
A person who supports the monarchy of a country.

sovereign (adjective)
Possessing supreme or ultimate power.

telegraph
A system for transmitting messages over a distance along a wire.

trade union
An organised association of workers in a trade or profession, formed to protect and further their rights and interests.

trench warfare
A type of combat in which opposing troops fight from trenches facing each other.

two-stroke piston engine
An engine that transmits power by one up-down movement of a piston (a cylinder containing a disc that is pushed up and down).

vaccine
A substance that gives immunity to a disease.

virus
A type of microorganism that can only reproduce inside a host cell.

FURTHER INFORMATION

Books

The British Empire (Great Empires)
Ellis Roxburgh
Wayland, 2017

Charles Darwin (History VIPs)
Kay Barnham
Wayland, 2017

Horrible Jobs of the Industrial Revolution (History's Most Horrible Jobs)
Leon Gray
Raintree, 2017

The Story of Lewis and Clark (Explorers)
Jacqueline Morley
Book House, 2017

The Victorians (All About)
Jane Goodwin

Websites

Explore the Industrial Revolution here: **www.bbc.co.uk/education/guides/zvmv4wx/revision**

Here you can find information on the French Revolution: **www.ducksters.com/history/french_revolution/**

Find out all about the events, battles and key figures of the American Civil War here: **www.ducksters.com/history/civil_war.php**

Here is some information on the Mexican war of independence: **wiki.kidzsearch.com/wiki/Mexican_War_of_Independence**

Learn about the colonisation of Africa here: encyclopedia.kids.net.au/page/co/Colonization_of_Africa#Early_modern

INDEX